First published in this format 2015

The Taunton Press
Inspiration for hands-on living®

The Taunton Press, Inc., 63 South Main Street
PO Box 5506, Newtown, CT 06470-5506

e-mail: tp@taunton.com

Text: Debby Ware
Interior Design: Deborah Kerner
Photographer: Alexandra Grablewski
Illustrators: Christine Erikson, Tinsley Morrison
Editor: Tim Stobierski
Copy Editor: Betty Christiansen

Threads® is a trademark of The Taunton Press, Inc.,
registered in the U.S. Patent and Trademark Office.

Library of Congress Cataloging-in-Publication Data

Ware, Debby, 1952-
  Seaside baby knits : nautical hats & sweaters to knit /
Debby Ware.
    pages cm. -- (Threads selects)
  ISBN 978-1-63186-314-1
1. Knitting--Patterns. 2. Infants' clothing. I. Title.
  TT825.W37286 2015
  746.43'20432--dc23
                              2015019706

Printed in the United States of America
10 9 8 7 6 5 4 3 2 1

CONTENTS

Luminous Lighthouse Hat

Let this hat lead your wandering sailor home. With a lining on the inside of the top, this lighthouse will stand tall and shed its light well.

Sizing

Small: 14-in. circumference

Large: 18-in. circumference

Figures for larger size are given in parentheses. Where only one set of figures appears, the directions apply to both sizes.

Yarn

DK weight smooth yarn

The hat shown is made with S.R. Kertzer Super 10 Cotton: 100% mercerized cotton, 4.4 oz. (125 g)/250 yd. (228.6 m).

Yardage

80 (100) yd. S.R. Kertzer Super 10 Cotton #0004 White

60 (80) yd. S.R. Kertzer Super 10 Cotton #3997 Scarlet

60 (80) yd. S.R. Kertzer Super 10 Cotton #0001 Black

40 (50) yd. S.R. Kertzer Super 10 Cotton #3553 Canary

Materials

16-in. U.S. size 4 (3.5 mm) circular needle

Four U.S. size 4 (3.5 mm) double-pointed needles

Stitch marker

Tapestry needle

GAUGE

22 sts = 4 in.

Directions

HAT BASE

With circ needles and Black, CO 90 (100) sts. Place a st marker on right needle and, beginning Rnd 1, join CO sts together making sure that sts do not become twisted on needle.

P2 rnds.

Attach White.

RIBBING

Make sure to keep unworked yarn in the back of your work.

*P2 with White, K2 with Black; rep from * to end of rnd.

Rep this ribbing rnd for a total of 8 rnds.

Drop White. With Black, K1 rnd. P2 rnds. Cut Black and attach Scarlet.

With Scarlet, K7 rnds.

Next Rnd: With Scarlet, *K8, K2tog; rep from * for entire rnd.

Drop Scarlet and pick up White.

With White, K7 rnds.

Next Rnd: *K7, K2tog; rep from * for entire rnd.

Continue in established pattern until you have completed a total of 4 Scarlet bands and have completed the last dec rnd of *K2, K2tog, placing sts on dpns when necessary.

Cut White.

RIDGE ROUND TO BEGIN LINING

With Scarlet, P1 rnd.

LINING

With Scarlet, knit lining until work measures 4 in. from Ridge Rnd.

BO all sts.

With Black and using dpns, evenly pick up sts along Ridge Rnd.

P2 rnds.

Attach Canary and rep ribbing as at base of hat, substituting Canary for White.

Work until ribbing measures 2 in. Cut Canary, and with Black, K1 rnd. P2 rnds. BO all sts.

LIGHT STREAKS

With Canary, create two 3-in. 3-st I-Cords (see p. 31).

FINISHING

Sew lining to inside of hat. Weave in all loose ends. Thread tapestry needle with CO ends of Canary I-cords and bring light streaks through top of hat, using photograph as reference. Weave in both CO and BO ends of each I-Cord.

Superb Sailor's Hat

This classic hat design is just what your little sailor needs when you're down on the pier admiring the boats.

Sizing

Small: 14-in. circumference

Large: 18-in. circumference

Figures for larger size are given in parentheses. Where only one set of figures appears, the directions apply to both sizes.

Yarn

DK weight smooth yarn

The hat shown is made with S.R. Kertzer Super 10 Cotton: 100% mercerized cotton, 4.4 oz. (125 g)/250 yd. (228.6 m)

Yardage

60 (80) yd. S.R. Kertzer Super 10 Cotton #0004 White

25 (30) yd. S.R. Kertzer Super 10 Cotton #3997 Scarlet

10 yd. S.R. Kertzer Super 10 Cotton #3873 Lapis

Materials

16-in. U.S. size 4 (3.5 mm) circular needle

Four U.S. size 4 (3.5 mm) double-pointed needles

Two stitch markers

Tapestry needle

GAUGE

22 sts = 4 in.

Directions

HAT BASE

With circ needles and Scarlet, CO 80 (100) sts. Place a st marker on right needle and, beginning Rnd 1, join CO sts together making sure that sts do not become twisted on needle.

P2 rnds.

Cut Scarlet and attach White. K all rnds until entire piece measures 2 in.

RIDGE ROUND

With White, P1 rnd.

Continue to knit all rnds until entire piece measures 4 in. Turn work "inside out," folding the piece at Ridge Rnd. The Scarlet cast-on rim should now be at the top of your work.

At the stitch marker, turn work and begin to knit.

K4 (2) rows. Place a second marker halfway around work at 40 (50) sts.

DECREASE ROUNDS

Continue with White, making the following decs on this and every row:

Knit to 2 sts before first marker, K1, sl 1, psso, sl marker, K2tog. Knit to 2 sts before second marker, K1, sl 1, psso, sl marker, K2tog.

Rep from * to * every rnd, placing sts on dpns when necessary until 38 (50) sts rem.

Place rem sts onto 2 dpns—19 (25) sts on each needle.

Using Three-Needle Bind-Off (see p. 31), BO rem sts.

FINISHING

Weave in all loose ends on wrong side of work.

Using Duplicate Stitch (see p. 30) and the photo as a guide, create an anchor decoration on the front of the hat or all around brim, if desired.

Adorable Anchor Cardigan

Every Seaside Baby needs a comfortable cotton cardigan for all those cool summer evenings! Partner this with the Superb Sailor's Hat (p. 5) for a complete, adorable ensemble.

Sizing

3–12 months: Chest: 20 in.
From shoulder to ribbing base: 10 in.

Yarn

DK weight smooth yarn

The sweater shown is made with S.R. Kertzer Super 10 Cotton: 100% mercerized cotton, 4.4 oz. (125 g)/250 yd. (228.6 m)

Yardage

150 yd. S.R. Kertzer Super 10 Cotton #0004 White

60 yd. S.R. Kertzer Super 10 Cotton #3997 Scarlet

40 yd. S.R. Kertzer Super 10 Cotton #3873 Lapis

Materials

One pair U.S. size 4 (3.5 mm) straight needles
16-in. U.S. size 4 (3.5 mm) circular needle
Two stitch holders
Tapestry needle

GAUGE

22 sts = 4 in.

This sweater is worked in one piece until it is divided at armhole openings.

Directions

RIBBING

With Lapis and straight needles, CO 120 sts. Work in Garter st (knit all rows) for 1½ in.

FOR THE CHECKERBOARD

Cut Lapis and **attach Scarlet. K2 rows.

Drop Scarlet and attach White. K2 rows.

Checkerboard Pattern: *K3 sts with White. Drop White and, with Scarlet, K3 sts*; rep from * to * for entire row.

P3 sts with Scarlet. Drop Scarlet and, with White, P3 sts; rep from * to * for entire row.

Drop Scarlet and K1 row and P1 row with White.

Drop White and, with Scarlet, K2 rows.**

Cut Scarlet and, with White, work Stockinette st for 2 in.

Drop White and attach Scarlet. K2 rows.

Rep Checkerboard Pattern.

With White, work 2 rows in Stockinette st.

Drop White and, with Scarlet, K2 rows.

DIVIDE FOR FRONTS

(WS) With White, P30 sts for right front; place next 60 sts onto holder to work later for back. Place rem 30 sts onto stitch holder for second front.

With White and working on 30 sts only, work Stockinette st for 2½ in.

NECK DECREASES

At neck edge, BO 8 sts at beg of next row. Knit to end of row.

P1 row.

At neck edge, BO 6 sts. Knit to end of row.

P1 row.

Continue working Stockinette st on rem 16 sts until entire work measures 12 in.

Place rem sts onto stitch holder. Cut yarn.

LEFT FRONT

Place 30 sts from stitch holder onto needle and work left front as right front, reversing shaping.

Place rem sts on stitch holder. Cut yarn.

BACK

Place rem 60 sts on needle and, with White, work Stockinette st until entire back measures 12 in.

SHOULDER SEAMS

Place 16 sts from left front onto needle. With RS of work facing, rejoin yarn and, using the Three-Needle Bind-Off (see p. 31), BO 16 sts, creating first shoulder seam.

Rep for 2nd shoulder.

Place rem 28 sts from back onto stitch holder.

SLEEVES

With RS facing and beginning at bottom of armhole, use Scarlet and 3 dpns to pick up approx 50 sts evenly around armhole. With Scarlet, P1 row.

Cut Scarlet and attach White. Continue to work in the round with White until entire sleeve measures 3 in. to 4 in.

Note: I like to keep sleeve lengths on the shorter side for babies (see the photo on p. 6). It helps to keep them out of food and other fun stuff! If you would like them longer, add the desired length here, before ribbing.

Rep Checkerboard Pattern from ** to **.

Cut Scarlet.

SLEEVE RIBBING

With White, K1 rnd.

Next Rnd: K2tog entire rnd.

Next Rnd*: K1, P1; rep from * for entire rnd.

Work 8 rnds ribbing total. BO all sts.

RIGHT FRONT BAND

With RS facing and with White, pick up approx 50 sts evenly along right front edge.

Ridge Row: P1 row. Continue in Stockinette st for 5 rows.

Create second Ridge Row for lining. Continue

in Stockinette st for 5 rows. BO all sts.

LEFT FRONT BAND

With RS facing, and with White, pick up approx
50–55 sts evenly along left front edge.

Ridge Row: P1 row.

Continue in Stockinette st for 1 row.

Buttonhole Row: Work 3 buttonholes as
follows:

Work to desired placement of first buttonhole,
BO 2 sts, work to desired placement
for second buttonhole, BO 2 sts, and
finally, work to desired placement for third
buttonhole, BO 2 sts.

Next Row: Work to buttonhole BO and CO
2 sts. Continue to CO 2 sts at rem created
buttonholes.

Work 2 rows in Stockinette st.

BO all sts purlwise.

NECKBAND

With RS facing and using Scarlet, pick up
approx 28 sts along right front neck edge,
work 28 sts on holder for back, and pick up
approx 28 sts along left front neck edge.

Next Row: K1 row.

Continue in Stockinette st for 5 rows.

RIDGE ROUND

*K2tog, yo; rep from * to end of row.

Continue in Stockinette st for 5 rows. BO all
sts. Cut yarn, leaving a long tail for finishing.

ANCHOR POCKET

With White and straight needles, co 20 sts.
Work in Stockinette st for 2 in.

Ridge Rnd: *K2, yo; rep from * for entire rnd.

Continue in Stockinette st for 2 in. BO all sts,
leaving a long tail for finishing pocket.

ANCHOR

With Lapis, and using Duplicate Stitch (see
p. 30), embroider anchor onto center front
of pocket.

Using long tail, sew pocket together along all
three edges of pocket. Attach pocket to right
side of cardigan with Ridge Row on top.

FINISHING

Turn neckband at Ridge Rnd and, using long
tail, sew down lining of band along neck
edge.

Weave in all loose ends on WS of work.

Attach 3 buttons.

Seashell Sun Bonnet

This wide-brimmed hat with decorative shells on top will keep the sun off your little one's face and look so sweet on the beach.

Sizing

One size: 20-in. circumference

Yarn

DK weight smooth yarn

The hat shown is made with S.R. Kertzer Super 10 Cotton: 100% mercerized cotton, 4.4 oz. (125 g)/250 yd. (228.6 m)

Yardage

70 yd. S.R. Kertzer Super 10 Cotton #0002 Cream

30 yd. S.R. Kertzer Super 10 Cotton #3533 Daffodil

50 yd. S.R. Kertzer Super 10 Cotton #3711 Honeydew

10 yd. S.R. Kertzer Super 10 Cotton #3446 Cotton Candy

Materials

16-in. U.S. size 4 (3.5 mm) circular needle

Four U.S. size 4 (3.5 mm) double-pointed needles

Stitch markers

Tapestry needle

GAUGE

22 sts = 4 in.

PICOT ROUND

With selected color, *K2, yo; rep from * for entire rnd.

This hat is knit from the crown down to the brim.

Directions

TOP OF BONNET

With Honeydew, CO 8 sts and divide evenly across 3 dpns. With 4th dpn, join to knit in the rnd.

Rnd 1: Kf&b 8 times (16 sts).

Rnd 2: K1f&b 16 times (32 sts).

Rnd 3: *K1, pm, K1f&b, K2*; rep from * to end (40 sts).

Rnd 4: *Knit to marker, sl marker, K1f&b*; rep from * to end of rnd (48 sts).

Rnd 5: Cut Honeydew and attach Cream. With Cream, knit to end.

Rep rnds 4 and 5 until you have 104 sts and 13 sts between each marker.

Drop Cream and attach Honeydew.

RIDGE ROUND

*With Honeydew, K1 rnd. P1 rnd.
Drop Honeydew and pick up Cream. K3 rnds.*
Rep from * to * for a total of 6 Honeydew Ridge
   Rnds.

BRIM RIDGE ROUND

Drop Honeydew and attach Daffodil.

Work K1, P1 ribbing for entire rnd. Rep ribbing
   for a total of 3 rnds.
Cut Daffodil, pick up Cream, and K1 rnd.

TOP BRIM

Rnd 1: *K to 1 st before marker, K1f&b, sl
   marker, K1f&b. Rep from * to end of rnd.
Rnd 2: Knit.

Rep these 2 rnds until you have 216 sts total
(27 sts between each marker).

Drop Cream.

With Daffodil, create Picot Rnd, removing all
markers as you knit.

Cut Daffodil and attach Honeydew.

BRIM LINING

Rnd 1: Knit all sts, placing a distinguishing
marker at the beginning of the rnd and
another marker after the first 14 sts. Then,
place a marker every 27 sts around brim.

Rnd 2: *K to 2 sts before marker, sl 1, K1,
psso, sl marker, K2tog*. Rep to end of rnd.

Note: Do not make decs at marker
designating start of rnd. (Make this marker
different than all the other markers to avoid
confusion.)

Rnd 3: Knit.

Rep Rnds 2 & 3 until 104 sts rem.

BO loosely, leaving a long tail.

SEASHELLS

Create 6 seashells, 3 each in Honeydew and
Cream.

CO 21 sts.

Row 1: Knit.

Row 2: P1, *K3, P1*; rep from * to * to end of
row.

Row 3: K1, *P3, K1*; rep from * to * to end of
row.

Row 4: P1, *K3, P1*; rep from * to * to end of
row.

Row 5: K1 *sl1 pwise, P1, psso, P1, K1*; rep
from * to * to end of row.

Row 6: P1 *K2, P1*; rep from * to * to end of
row.

Row 7: K1, *sl1 pwise, P1, psso, K1*; rep
from * to * to end of row.

Row 8: P1, *K1, P1*; rep from * to * to end of
row.

Row 9: K1, *K2tog to end of row.

Row 10: P1, sl next 4 sts onto dpn.
Wrap yarn around the 4 sts on dpn
counterclockwise 3 times. Slip 4 sts back
onto working needle, P1.

Row 11: Knit.

Row 12: *P1, M1 pwise, P1, M1 pwise, P1,
M1 pwise, P1, M1 pwise. End K1.

Row 13: *K2, K1f&b*; rep from * to * to end of
row. End K1.

Row 14: BO all sts kwise

CROWN WELT

Thread a tapestry needle with Honeydew
and pinch the hat at the first Ridge Row
on crown and create a Welt (see p. 31) by
sewing together the top and bottom pieces
using even running sts.

Using CO end, attach each seashell firmly at
the base, alternating colors, on top of crown
at Welt edge, letting them stand up.

FINISHING

Using the long tail, sew the BO edge to the
bottom of the band on the inside of the hat.

Weave in all loose ends on inside of hat.

Splish-Splashing Sailboat Beanie

With waves splashing all around, this beanie is ready to go wherever your little one will sail it!

Sizing

Small: 14-in. circumference

Large: 18-in. circumference

Figures for larger size are given in parentheses. Where only one set of figures appears, the directions apply to both sizes.

Yarn

DK weight smooth yarn

The hat shown is made with S.R. Kertzer Super 10 Cotton: 100% mercerized cotton, 4.4 oz. (125 g)/250 yd. (228.6 m)

Yardage

80 (100) yd. S.R. Kertzer Super 10 Cotton #3532 Soft Yellow

20 (30) yd. S.R. Kertzer Super 10 Cotton #3841 Caribbean

5 (10) yd. S.R. Kertzer Super 10 Cotton #3533 Daffodil

5 (10) yd. S.R. Kertzer Super 10 Cotton #3711 Honeydew

1 yd. S.R. Kertzer Super 10 Cotton #3997 Scarlet

Materials

16-in. U.S. size 4 (3.5 mm) circular needle

One pair U.S. size 4 (3.5 mm) straight needles

Four U.S. size 4 (3.5 mm) double-pointed needles

Stitch marker

Tapestry needle

Small amount of polyester filling

GAUGE

22 sts = 4 in.

SEED STITCH

Rnd 1: *K1, P1; rep from * to end of rnd.

All other rnds: Knit the purl sts and purl the knit sts.

Directions

With circ needles and Soft Yellow, CO 80 (100) sts. Place a st marker on right needle and, beginning Rnd 1, join CO sts together making sure that sts do not become twisted on needle.

P1 rnd.

Continue in Seed st until entire piece measures 6 (7) in.

Next and Following Rnds: K2tog, placing sts on dpns when necessary, until approx 10 sts rem. Cut a long tail, thread tail through tapestry needle, and thread needle through rem sts on needle. Pull tightly and bring yarn to WS of work.

SAILBOAT

This boat is made in one piece and is folded in half at Ridge Row.

With Daffodil and straight needles, CO 15 (25) sts. K1 row, P1 row.

Row 1 and All Odd Rows: K2tog, K to last 2 sts, K2tog.

Row 2 and All Even Rows: P.

Work as established until 5 (15) sts rem.

Ridge Row (WS): K.

Row 1 and All Odd Rows: Kf&b, K to last st, Kf&b.

Row 2 and All Even Rows: P.

Work as established until there are 15 (25) sts. BO all sts.

SAIL

Make 2.

With Honeydew and straight needles, CO 15 (25) sts.

Row 1 and All Odd Rows: K2tog, K to last 2 sts, K2tog.

Row 2 and All Even Rows: P.

Work as established (creating a triangle) until 3 sts rem. Sl1, p2tog, psso.

OCEAN WAVES

With Caribbean and straight needles, CO 3 sts.

*Row 1: K2, yo, K1.

Row 2: K4 sts.

Row 3: K3, yo, K1.

Row 4: K5 sts.

Row 5: K4, yo, K1.

Row 6: K6 sts.

Row 7: K5, yo, K1.

Row 8: BO 4 sts.*

Rep from * to * until you have created a piece long enough to sew to bottom rim of beanie. (If desired, create 2 sets of waves for the larger size beanie. Sew one at the rim and one at the peak around the sailboat.)

SMALL RED FLAG

With Scarlet and straight needles, CO 2 (4) sts. Kf&b&f of each st.

Next Row: BO all sts.

FINISHING

To help sailboat stay "afloat," fill sailboat and sail with a small amount of polyester filling.

Sew up seams to sailboat and sail.

Attach sailboat to peak of beanie. Attach sail to sailboat.

Attach small flag to peak of sail.

Roll brim of hat up toward top of hat until you have a 2-in.-wide brim.

Using a running st, sew ocean waves to edge of hat base.

Boatneck Summer Sweater

Slip this easy-fitting sweater onto your little one. The ocean's waves and sailboat are an easily created adornment, and pair well with the beanie on p. 16.

Sizing

3–6 months: Chest: 24 in.
From shoulder to ribbing base: 10 in.

Yarn

DK weight smooth yarn

The sweater shown is made with S.R. Kertzer Super 10 Cotton: 100% mercerized cotton, 4.4 oz. (125 g)/250 yd. (228.6 m)

Yardage

40 yd. S.R. Kertzer Super 10 Cotton #3533 Daffodil

80 yd. S.R. Kertzer Super 10 Cotton #3841 Caribbean

40 yd. S.R. Kertzer Super 10 Cotton #3711 Honeydew

2 yd. S.R. Kertzer Super 10 Cotton #3997 Scarlet

300 yd. S.R. Kertzer Super 10 Cotton #3532 Soft Yellow

Materials

32-in. U.S. size 4 (3.5 mm) circular needle

16-in. U.S. size 4 (3.5 mm) circular needle

Five U.S. size 4 (3.5 mm) double-pointed needles

Stitch marker

Tapestry needle

GAUGE

22 sts = 4 in.

This sweater is knit in the round until it is divided at armhole openings.

Directions

RIBBING

With circ needles and Daffodil, CO 150 sts. Place a st marker on right needle and, beginning Rnd 1, join CO sts together making sure that sts do not twist on needle.

P1 rnd.

Attach Honeydew. *With Daffodil K1, with Honeydew P1; keeping unworked yarn in the back of your work, continue from * for entire rnd.

Continue in established ribbing until entire piece measures 1½ in. Cut Honeydew and, with Daffodil, K1 rnd, P1 rnd. Cut Daffodil and attach Caribbean.

K all rnds until you have completed 3 in. of Caribbean.

Cut Caribbean and attach Soft Yellow.

Work until entire piece measures 6 in. from beginning of ribbing.

DIVIDE FOR ARMHOLES

Place 75 sts on another needle or stitch holder for back of sweater.

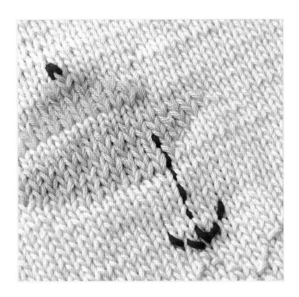

Front: Work on the rem 75 sts back and forth in Stockinette st until entire piece measures 10 in., ending with completed WS row.

BOATNECK

K10 sts, BO 55 sts, K10 sts.

Place rem sts from front on another needle.

Back: Rep as front.

SHOULDERS

Placing rem 10 sts on each shoulder together with WS facing. Create seams using Three-Needle Bind-Off (see p. 31).

SLEEVES

Beginning at bottom of armhole, with Soft Yellow and 16-in. circular needle, pick up 54 sts evenly around armhole opening. Work in the round until entire sleeve measures 5 in., or desired length.

SLEEVE CUFF

K1, K2tog; * rep for entire rnd, placing sts on dpns when necessary.

Work K1, P1 ribbing for 1 in. BO all sts.

FINISHING

Weave in all loose ends.

OCEAN SCENE

Using photograph for reference, create the following on front of sweater:

Sailboat: Thread a tapestry needle with Honeydew and, using Duplicate Stitch (see p. 30), create the hull of the boat by starting at bottom and working approx 7 sts across center left of front of sweater. Work 1 more st on each side on each row until you have 7 rows.

Weave in all loose ends on WS.

Thread a tapestry needle with Daffodil and, using Duplicate Stitch, create the sail by working 3 rows above top of hull and working 11 sts across bottom row. Decrease 1 st each side until you have created a small triangle and 3 sts rem on top.

Thread a tapestry needle with Scarlet and, using Duplicate Stitch, create a flag on top of sail by working 1 st on top of sail.

Anchor: Thread a tapestry needle with Scarlet and, beginning at center right side, create approx 6 small running sts down front of sweater. Create the shape of a small anchor by making 2 small running sts on each side.

Waves: Thread a tapestry needle with Caribbean and, using a small running st, create small peaks of waves across front of sweater beginning at top of knitted Caribbean row. The waves can be as high or low as you wish and can either peak straight, bend right, or bend left. Use your imagination!

Hot Lobster Pot Top

Seems that there are lobsters in this lobster pot! This top hat stands tall with a white checkerboard border and lots of claws for everyone!

Sizing

One size: 18-in. to 20-in. circumference

Yarn

DK weight smooth yarn

The hat shown is made with S.R. Kertzer Super 10 Cotton: 100% mercerized cotton, 4.4 oz. (125 g)/250 yd. (228.6 m)

Yardage

100 yd. S.R. Kertzer Super 10 Cotton #3533 Daffodil

50 yd. S.R. Kertzer Super 10 Cotton #0004 White

10 yd. S.R. Kertzer Super 10 Cotton #3997 Scarlet

Materials

16-in. U.S. size 4 (3.5 mm) circular needle

Four U.S. size 4 (3.5 mm) double-pointed needles

Stitch marker

Tapestry needle

GAUGE

22 sts = 4 in.

Directions

HAT BASE

With circ needles and Daffodil, CO 100 sts. Place a st marker on right needle and, beginning Rnd 1, join CO sts together making sure that sts do not become twisted on needle.

P1 rnd.

Knit all rnds until entire piece measures 2½ in.

CHECKERBOARD

Attach White and work the following pattern:

With White K5, with Daffodil K5; rep from * to * for entire rnd.

Continue in established pattern for a total of 5 rnds.

With Daffodil K5, with White K5; rep from * to * for entire rnd.

Continue in established pattern for a total of 5 rnds.

Cut White and, with Daffodil, K until entire piece measures 7 in.

RIDGE ROUND FOR LINING

P1 rnd.

TOP LINING

Continue to K for another 2 in. BO all sts.

CROWN

With RS facing, pick up 100 sts around BO
end of lining. K10 rnds.

CROWN DECREASE ROUNDS

Rnd 1: *K8, K2tog*; rep from * to * for entire
rnd

Rnd 2: *K7, K2tog*; rep from * to * for entire
rnd.

Continue in established pattern, placing sts on
dpns when necessary, until approx 6 sts

rem. Cut yarn, leaving a 6-in. tail. Thread a
tapestry needle and pass needle through
rem sts on needle. Pull tightly and bring
needle to WS of work and fasten off.

FINISHING

Turn lining at Ridge Row. Thread a tapestry
needle with White and create a small running
st along peak of hat.

Weave in all loose ends.

With Scarlet and using Duplicate Stitch (see
p. 30), decorate your lobster pot with claws
all around using the photo as reference.

Beach Glass Beanie

All those beautiful colors you find on the seashore are all wrapped up in this beach beanie with plenty of pastel squiggles on top.

Sizing

Small: 16-in. circumference

Large: 20-in. circumference

Figures for larger size are given in parentheses. Where only one set of figures appears, the directions apply to both sizes.

Yarn

DK weight smooth yarn

The hat shown is made with S.R. Kertzer Super 10 Cotton: 100% mercerized cotton, 4.4 oz. (125 g)/250 yd. (228.6 m)

Yardage

50 (60) yd. S.R. Kertzer Super 10 Cotton #0004 White

40 yd. S.R. Kertzer Super 10 Cotton #3533 Daffodil

40 yd. S.R. Kertzer Super 10 Cotton #3446 Cotton Candy

40 yd. S.R. Kertzer Super 10 Cotton #3841 Caribbean

40 yd. S.R. Kertzer Super 10 Cotton #3711 Honeydew

Materials

16-in. U.S. size 4 (3.5 mm) circular needle

Four U.S. size 4 (3.5 mm) double-pointed needles

Stitch marker

Tapestry needle

GAUGE

22 sts = 4 in.

PICOT ROUND

With selected color, *K2, yo; rep from * for entire rnd.

COLORFUL SQUIGGLES

Using Cable Cast-On (see p. 30), CO 8 sts with desired color. Immediately BO 8 sts.

Directions

HAT BASE

With circ needles and White, CO 90 (100) sts. Place a st marker on right needle and, beginning Rnd 1, join CO sts together making sure that sts do not become twisted on needle.

P1 rnd.

K10 rnds.

FIRST PICOT ROUND

Drop White, attach Daffodil, and create Picot Rnd.

Next Rnd: Cut Daffodil, pick up White, and
K4 rnds.

Next Rnd: Drop White, attach Honeydew,
and create second Picot Rnd.

Next Rnd: Cut Honeydew, pick up White, and
K4 rnds.

Next Rnd: Drop White, attach Caribbean, and
create third Picot Rnd.

Next Rnd: Cut Caribbean, pick up White, and
K4 rnds.

Next Rnd: Drop White, attach Cotton Candy,
and create fourth Picot Rnd.

Next Rnd: Cut Cotton Candy, pick up White,
and K4 rnds.

Next Rnd: Rep first Picot Rnd with Daffodil.

Next Rnd: Cut Daffodil, pick up White, and
K4 rnds.

RIDGE ROUNDS

Drop White and attach Honeydew. K1 rnd, P1
rnd.

Drop Honeydew and attach Caribbean. K1 rnd,
P1 rnd.

Drop Caribbean and attach Cotton Candy. K1
rnd, P1 rnd.

Drop Cotton Candy and pick up Honeydew. K1
rnd, P1 rnd.

With White, K4 rnds.

FIRST SQUIGGLE ROUND

*With White K4 sts. Drop White and attach
Daffodil, and on the next st create Squiggle.

Drop Daffodil and pick up White. With White,
BO the final Daffodil st that is on the right
needle.* Rep from * to * for entire rnd.

Cut Daffodil and, with White, K4 rnds.

SECOND SQUIGGLE ROUND

*With White, K3 sts. Drop White and attach
Honeydew, and on the next st create
Squiggle. Drop Honeydew and pick up
White. With White, BO the final Honeydew st
that is on the right needle.* Rep from * to *
for entire rnd.

Cut Honeydew and, with White, K4 rnds.

Rep established Squiggle Rnd pattern with
Caribbean and Cotton Candy.

After completing final Squiggle Rnd with Cotton
Candy, pick up White and K2 rnds.

Next Rnd: K2tog entire rnd.

Cut yarn, leaving approx 8-in. tail.

Thread a tapestry needle with the tail and pass
needle through rem sts on needle. Pull
thread tightly and bring tail to WS of work.

FINISHING

Weave in all loose ends on WS of work.

Abbreviations

approx	approximately	K2tog	knit 2 stitches together
beg	beginning	P	purl
BO	bind off	rem	remaining
circ	circular	rep	repeat
CO	cast on	rnd	round
cont	continue	RS	right side
dec	decrease/decreases/ decreasing	sl 1	slip 1 stitch
dpn(s)	double-pointed needle(s)	st(s)	stitch(es)
inc	increase/increases/ increasing	St st	stockinette stitch
		tog	together
K	knit	WS	wrong side
K1f&b	knit in the front and in the back of the same stitch	yd	yard/yards
		YO	yarn over

Standard Yarn Weights

NUMBERED BALL	DESCRIPTION	STS/4 IN.	NEEDLE SIZE
1 SUPER FINE	Sock, baby, fingering	27–32	2.25–3.25 mm (U.S. 1–3)
2 FINE	Sport, baby	23–26	3.25–3.75 mm (U.S. 3–5)
3 LIGHT	DK, light worsted	21–24	3.75–4.5 mm (U.S. 5–7)
4 MEDIUM	Worsted, afghan, Aran	16–20	4.5–5.5 mm (U.S. 7–9)
5 BULKY	Chunky, craft, rug	12–15	5.5–8.0 mm (U.S. 9–11)
6 SUPER BULKY	Bulky, roving	6–11	8 mm and larger (U.S. 11 and larger)

Special Stitches

Cable Cast-On

Insert right needle between first 2 sts on left needle. Wrap yarn as if to knit. Draw yarn through to complete st and slip this new st onto left needle.

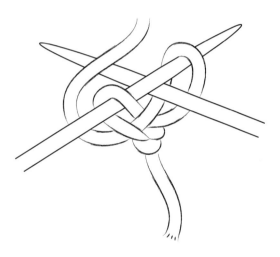

Duplicate Stitch

Thread a tapestry needle with the desired color yarn. Bring the needle through from the WS of the work to the base of the knit st you wish to cover with a duplicate st on the front side. Insert the needle directly under the base of the knit st that lies above the st you wish to cover. Bring the needle down and insert it at the base of the same knit st. Bring the tip of the needle out at the base of the next st you wish to cover and repeat this process until you have covered all the desired sts in the design.

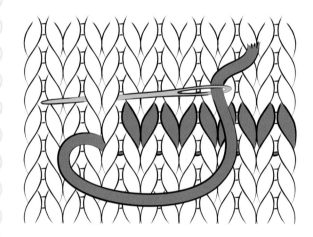

Special Stitches

I-Cord

With two dpns, work I-Cord as follows: K 4 to 6 sts. *Do not turn work. Slide sts to other end of needle, pull the yarn around the back, and knit the sts as usual. Repeat from * for desired length of cord.

Three-Needle Bind-Off

With right sides of work facing each other, hold needles parallel in your left hand, with the same number of sts on each needle. Hold the third needle in your right hand. *Insert third needle knitwise into both the first st on the needle closest to you and the first st of the back needle. K those 2 sts together. That st is now on the right needle.* Repeat from * to *. Using the tip of one of the needles in your left hand, pass the first st worked over the second st to bind off. Repeat across the row.

Welt

Create a small welt by passing the needle over and under the pieces of knitting that you have "pinched" together, for example, at the side and the crown of the hat. Weave both pieces (the side and the crown) together using evenly spaced running sts that are approx ¼ in. from the crown edge. Sewing the two pieces together in this way will create a slight thickening or "welt" along the edge of the crown.